Jean Paul GAULTIER

Translated from the French by Jane Brenton

First Published in Great Britain in 1996
by Thames and Hudson Ltd, London

Copyright © Éditions Assouline

British Library Cataloguing-in-Publication Data

A catalogue record for this book is available from the British Library

ISBN 0-500-01755-7

Printed and bound in Italy

Jean Paul GAULTIER

TEXT BY FARID CHENOUNE

THAMES AND HUDSON

When someone comes to write a history of manners – good and bad, graces and disgraces – of the latter third of this century, he should certainly take a look inside Jean-Paul Gaultier's gallery of fashion. There he will find full-lipped enchantresses, little hats at a jaunty angle on their heads, slipping on seven-league boots, zipping the hips of fitted coats that are also jogging suits, and magically sprouting breasts that look for all the world like velvet bombshells. He will find bewitching boys with legs encased in mesh stockings; New Age squaws wearing eighteenth-century tunics, flesh and fabric bodies tattooed, majestically displaying some ceremonial attribute of neopunk body-piercing; camp body-builders wrapped in voile jackets; whiplash Parisiennes, corseted, laced and fishnetted, in sleek suits and stretch lace; male princesses in bustiers with trains; geishas in black bomber jackets with long hobble skirts; Tyrolean girls with blonde plaits and glowing cheeks; sixties dollies; forties concierges; Juliette Grécos; leather women; silk and muslin men. And, finally, amid all this display of exaggerated beauties – one of the definitions of fashion, incidentally – he will find the little devil himself, Gaultier as his official image always portrays him: round head, platinum crop, striped sailor top, kilt bobbing over jeans or black Lycra tights, feet clad in Doc Marten boots, like some bizarrely outfitted globetrotter setting out to explore the world.

This year, said Tristouse, fashion is strange yet familiar, it is simple and yet fantastic. All the materials from the different realms of nature can now be employed in the composition of a woman's outfit. I saw a charming dress made entirely of corks. It was every bit the equal of the delightful evening dresses in washable fabrics that are the rage at premières [...]. Fishbones are much worn on hats [...]. Porcelain, stonewear and china have suddenly become part of the sartorial art. These materials are worn in belts, on hatpins, etc. [...]. Not to mention dresses decorated with oil paints, woollens in lurid colours, dresses oddly spattered with ink [...]. Walnut-shells make pretty pendants, especially if you add a few hazelnuts as well. A dress embroidered with coffee grains and cloves, onions, cloves of garlic and bunches of grapes will be acceptable wear for visiting. Fashion is becoming practical, ruling out nothing and ennobling everything. Fashion is doing for materials what the Romantics did for words.

Guillaume Apollinaire, *Le Poète assassiné*, 1911–13

fashion encourages imaginary genealogies: suppose that in the thirties Apollinaire had whispered his frivolous philosophy into Schiaparelli's ear, and 'Schiap' listened to what he had to say (she was after all to make a hat out of a shoe) and then, in the fifties, she in turn had a quiet word with Cardin. It was, after all, with Pierre Cardin that Jean-Paul Gaultier started his career at the age of eighteen, in the early months of 1970, working as an assistant and slaving away at his sketches. Cardin, who with Yves Saint Laurent was one of the rare couturiers who attempted to convey in his designs the spirit of the age, and who handed down to Gaultier the message that anything was possible, nothing was set in stone – 'there is absolutely no reason why you cannot make a shoe out of a scrap of fabric picked up off the ground'.[1] This art of recycling cast-offs (the collection as collection) was to become a fundamental principle of Gaultier's approach.

After a short time with Jacques Esterel in 1971 and two years with Patou struggling to come to terms with the timidity of a fashion house still stuck firmly in the past – no coloured models (no one used the word 'black' in those days) so as not to offend the American clientele – he returned to work for Pierre Cardin, who sent him to Manilla to design various minor collections for the American market. In those years in which Jean-Paul Gaultier was finding his way in the world of fashion, haute couture was like a magnificent ruined city, with crumbling piles of tulle, faille and organza, inhabited by legendary shades of a past elegance whose conventions remained frozen, impervious to changing times, gestures and attitudes. The Chanel–Courrèges confrontation of the sixties was long forgotten. But in society overall, there were rumblings: the oil crisis, revelations of the Soviet gulag, the final dashing of revolutionary and communitarian hopes founded in the events of May 1968 and hippie culture. In October 1976, at the Palais de la Découverte, Gaultier launched his first collection, displaying his woven straw 'tablemat' dresses to a bemused public. In the wider world, the talk was of deepening crisis, and on the other side of the Channel the Sex Pistols and the punks desecrated English brick walls with anti-social graffiti proclaiming the young generation's war-cry of 'no future!'

for Jean-Paul Gaultier, the bizarre world that was London in the post-punk era – Portobello Market, the King's Road, black-clad 'concierges' with green hair – demonstrated to perfection street fashion's talent for mix and match, and offered him a rich vein of inspiration. As if to announce he had gone over to the enemy, complete with needles and scissors, he chose as the musical accompaniment for the wide-brimmed hats and leatherette pants of his 'James Bond' collection the Sex Pistols' 'Destroy', a raucous version of Frank Sinatra's classic 'My Way', not so much a musical accessory as a fashion manifesto. That was in 1979. Only a year after its opening, in March 1978, the Palace, former music-hall venue used subsequently as disco and shrine of Paris night-life, had already welcomed hundreds of thousands inside its doors. Fashion was in the throes of becoming fashionable, with Jean-Paul Gaultier as its *enfant terrible*, to use the epithet shortly to be pinned on him. 'Gaul'tier', as his fans were to call him, emphasizing the 'I' (perhaps to distinguish him from the distinguished writer Théophile?), had found his method: collect, convert, combine. His approach represented the convergence of a number of different traditions: that of the ateliers of haute couture, formerly fashion's highest court of appeal, and that of the street, the latest arbiter of modishness, but also, in between past and present, the tradition of the flea market, that anonymous university of style in which Gaultier, like the rest of his generation, would hunt out clothes, fabrics and cuts impossible to find elsewhere, acquiring as he rummaged through piles of about the whys and wherefores of fashion. Upset by the interrogation, the victim racks his brains, sweats blood and tears and gets himself tied up in knots, mumbling a series of contradictory rehearsed responses, while feverishly turning out sketches that end up in the waste-paper basket. What gets him off the hook in the end is a frenetic ballet involving scissors and models, the uncoordinated display or collage mirroring the random nature of the clothes.

The frills and furbelows women deck themselves out in, and cheap trinkets covered in decoration, these have always held a peculiar fascination for me. A friend of mine used to collect anything of this sort he could lay hands on. Hidden away in a mahogany box he had a black silk band, the edge of which was decorated with very fine lace and sequins made of paste. It must have come from an old ball gown; in places, the silk was stained with mildew. I used to give him stamps or even money in order to be allowed a look at it. He would take me into a little old-fashioned salon while his parents were asleep and show it to me. I would stand there, the piece of silk in my hand, dumb with wonder and delight.

Marcel Blecher,
Aventures dans l'irréalité immédiate, 1936

Swapping around the identities of garments leads one straight into the eye of the storm as far as contemporary fashion is concerned: in other words, to the tension between masculine and feminine genres. Of all the designers of his generation, it is indisputably Jean-Paul Gaultier who has dressed, decorated and disguised in the most spectacular fashion that ambivalent figure who exists somewhere between the two. Without going too deeply into a complex area of history that still remains to be written, suffice it to say that, if Gaultier's age finds him so disturbing, it is partly because he has projected onto fashion and found design equivalents of the continuing reverberations of two particular cultural trends with their roots in the seventies: the feminist movement and, perhaps even more significantly, homosexual coming-out.

By the beginning of the eighties, women's liberation seemed a spent force. Having reached the peak of its influence ten years earlier, it now seemed old-hat, an unfashionable cause rarely referred to unless obliquely, as in the 1984 hit by Cookie Dingler, a sweetly fierce little song with the refrain: 'Don't drop her/ She's so fragile/ Being a liberated woman/ Isn't easy.' High heels, suspender belts, silk underwear, low-cut bras, women were reclaiming as their own the most classic elements of conventionally sexy gear, and no one, or almost no one, saw it as representing a reversion to sexism. As for the homosexual movement, it was in its heyday, basking in general acceptance: the widespread use of the word 'gay' was the outward sign of open tolerance and, on 19 December 1979, the first Gay Party was held at the Palace in Paris by its founder, Fabrice Emaer.

Jean-Paul Gaultier likes to represent himself as an interpreter of his age. But unlike other rather more bowdlerized interpretations of these social tendencies, such as the stylized 'temptress' invented by Chantal Thomass or the image of the male clothes-horse promoted by off-the-peg fashion, his contributions appear to come from the full and unexpurgated text. In dressing his age, he contrives also to strip it bare. In 1984, in a parody of the rhetoric of the female sex-object, he presented his first collection for men under the title 'The Male Object', and in

Spring/Summer 1985 ('And God Created Woman') he launched his 'skirt for men'. Here Gaultier touched on a fundamental aspect of our Western attitude towards appearances, a sexual dimorphism dictating one set of clothes for men and another for women. In practice this has always been a highly sensitive area for, although the female and the male wardrobes are distinct, the former has since the eighteenth century and beyond been accustomed to borrow from the latter, adopting frock coat, jacket, waistcoat, tie and later also trousers, so enjoying all the advantages of an entire new range of clothing without abandoning its own distinctive styles and prerogatives. At the end of the nineteenth century, Rachilde, author of *Monsieur Vénus*, had to obtain a permit from the prefect to be allowed to attend to her business as a journalist dressed in men's clothing.[2] Nowadays, no passport is needed for women to cross at will from one side of the anatomical divide to the other.

Of course, even the tiniest alterations would be significant, all the subtle ways in which these masculine garments were transformed as they were incorporated into the female wardrobe (and here it is interesting to note that, with Gaultier, women's jackets retain the same style of buttoning as men's); such an awareness ought presumably to modify the general perception of the divide between the sexes. Yet for the male world, crossing that divide remained taboo, and the clinching argument that perpetuated a ridiculously unequal state of affairs was the idea of a man in a skirt. Yet, like the bermudas/skirt of Jacques Esterel in 1966, Jean-Paul Gaultier's skirt for men was not in fact a skirt, it was a pair of trousers, one leg of which lapped over the other, more in the fashion of a loincloth. The transgression was no more than apparent, but the illusion (like all the best fashion illusions when they are effective) perfectly fulfilled its role as provocation, stimulating and focusing the debate then current about the respective identities of the two sexes. The unisex of the early seventies had tended rather to blur the distinction between the two.

g aultier played with an explosive mixture ('Une Garde-robe pour Deux', 1985) of sizzling high-tension promiscuities, each sex invited to explore and exploit, play with and enjoy, its own and the other's clichés. Postfeminist women, or girls (in the eighties the term had lost its stigma), preened in black leather lingerie and red lace, swanked in evening suit and corset, paraded in slinky frocks with 'buttock' cut-outs. Men, or more accurately boys, postphallocratic and macho, advanced lasciviously on platform-soled basket-ball boots, pushing out their chests in low-backed sweaters, shrugging their shoulders inside open-necked furs, adopting the little-hat-with-veil pose, now as 'homme fatal', now 'pretty boy', 'French gigolo', 'rock star', 'Robin Hood of the city', 'urban cowboy' or 'couture man'. This superabundance of clichés, this magically sly approach to fashion, treating it like a deliberate lapse of taste or as though the whole thing was some ghastly mistake, was greeted by the audience with laughter and whistles. It was exciting. In a simplified form, it provided the basis for the outfit Gaultier designed for Madonna's world tour in 1990: a man's dark suit worn over a salmon-pink corset, an outfit that he believed summed up the contemporary world. 'The bust pokes through the jacket, it is power and sensuality combined,' he declared.[3] A jacket, a corset, but also a pin-striped suit, a fitted coat, pyjama-style trousers, a catsuit, a bomber jacket: the simplicity and classicism of these key designs running through his collections would be seized on by press and public alike, appreciative of the care that went into their manufacture and finishing: the cloth of the

13

lining that is a rather more than just a lining, the buttonhole on the sleeve that prides itself on being a real buttonhole, the little overcast seam (called at Gaultier's, in a gallicized Italian, a *travette*) marking the corner of a pocket, stopping a dart or finishing a seam. Often praised as indicating a reassuringly commonsense attitude (a garment is after all made to be worn and ought to be reliable), Jean-Paul Gaultier's disciplined technique is also a relic of his nostalgia for haute couture, as he experienced it at first hand during the years of his apprenticeship and as it figured in his adolescent dreams.

e ven beyond haute couture, one can detect in Gaultier's work a sort of fetishistic or kitsch archaeology of feminine artifice and apparel. The territory he excavates is his own memory of the past, his feelings as a small boy in the fifties and sixties, raised in the suburbs, discovering the liturgy of femininity from magazines and from his guardian angel, the grandmother responsible for his initiation into these arcane mysteries. The whiff of rice powder that intoxicated his childhood, the reek of make-up, the fragrance of cleansers and varnish removers, of just these scents is his eau de toilette redolent, its liquid contained within a bottle shaped like a naked female torso; as too that torso and the frosted glass corset in which it is encased are redolent of the tales told him by his grandmother of turn-of-the-century women laced so tightly it made them faint. It was this childhood spent in the orbit of his grey-haired enchantress in closed rooms where 'things were yellowed by the sun'[4] that he also believed lay behind his palette of powdery pastels, burnt shades of sepia, peach, mustard, bottle green, chocolate, orange, rust, old rose, salmon pink, banana, colours that make his clothes appear slightly faded, with the headiness of a scent that has begun to go off. With Gaultier, fashion is subordinated to the spell cast by a personal history, it is viewed through the coloured filters of a photo love story. Indeed this genre of minor literature, hugely popular in the fifties, was something he experimented with himself, in *A Nous deux la mode!*, published in 1990, which tells the autobiographical story of a humorous young man who is fascinated by fashion and determined to come to grips with his passion.

but at the heart of all this constellation of idols lies Paris. Wherever his travels in transcouture may take him, Gaultier always returns to Paris. Whether the cosmopolitan streets of Barbès, the Pigalle of the cancan and Toulouse-Lautrec posters, the animated boulevards inhabited by Arletty in *Les Enfants du paradis*, 'le Paname' dancing to Yvette Horner's accordion, it is Paris that is the capital of his obsessions, the muse of his enduring themes. The Parisienne whom Jean-Paul Gaultier imagined in his Summer 1995 collection, with her 'gestures from a past age', her 'one gloved hand clasping the other glove', her 'high heels enhancing her legs',[5] she represents the distillation of a personal store of images that he both venerates and delights to shatter, at once idolater and iconoclast.

Paris, Place Clichy, 1 April 1996

Notes

1. *Paris-Match*, 24 April 1986.
2. Christine Bard, *Les Filles de Marianne. Histoire des féminismes 1914–1940*, Fayard, 1995, p. 200.
3. *Elle*, 21 March 1990.
4. *Beaux-Arts*, October 1993.
5. *Marie-Claire*, February 1995.

JEAN PAUL GAULTIER
PRÉSENTE

Gaultier

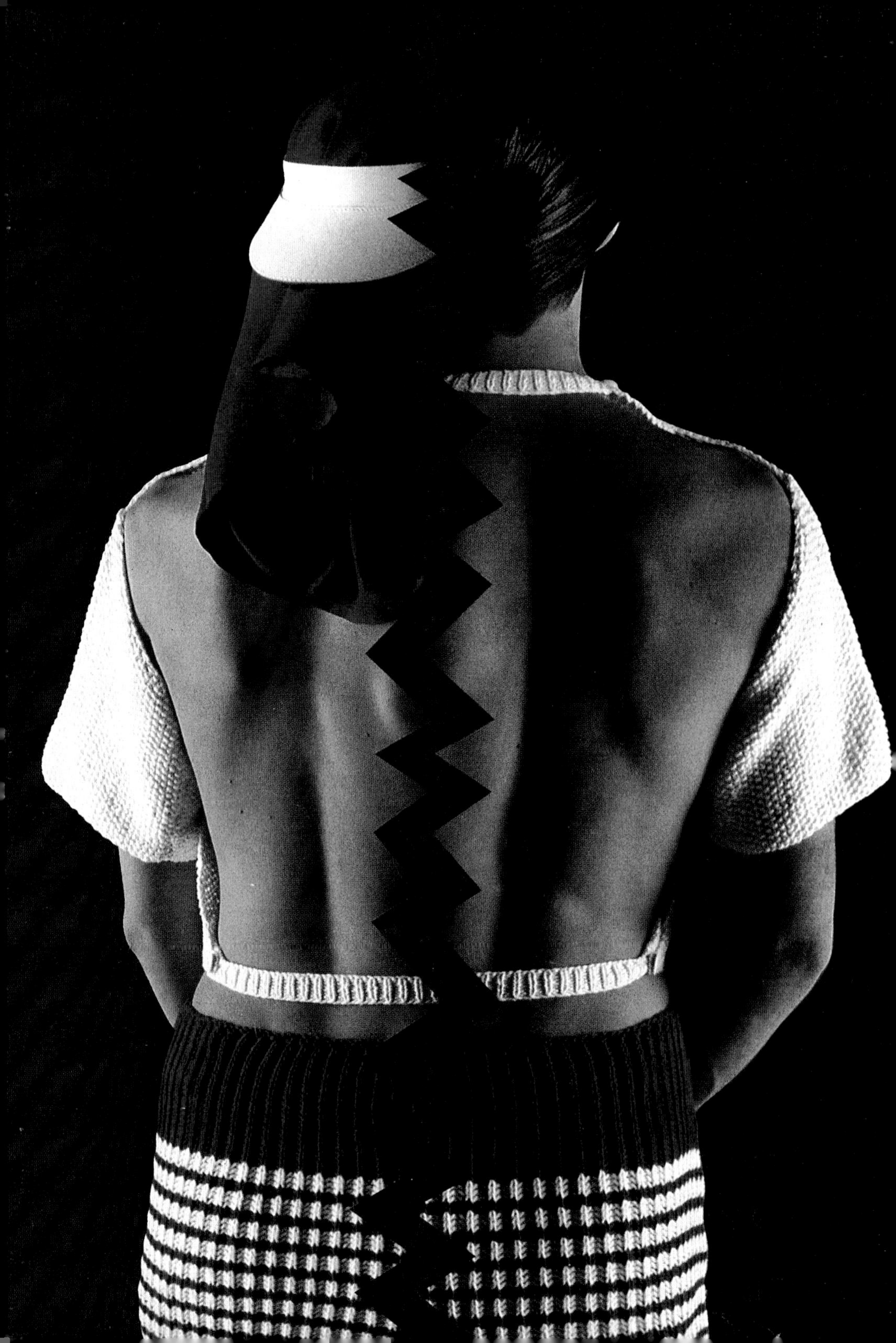

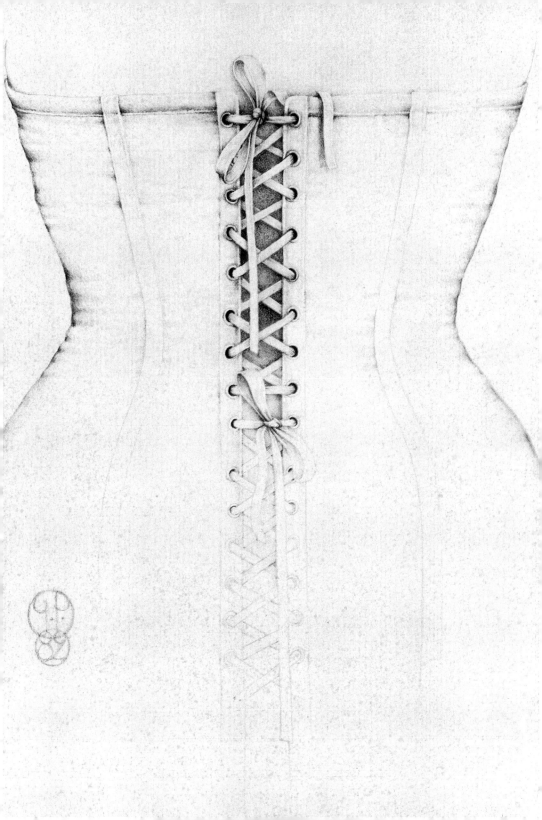

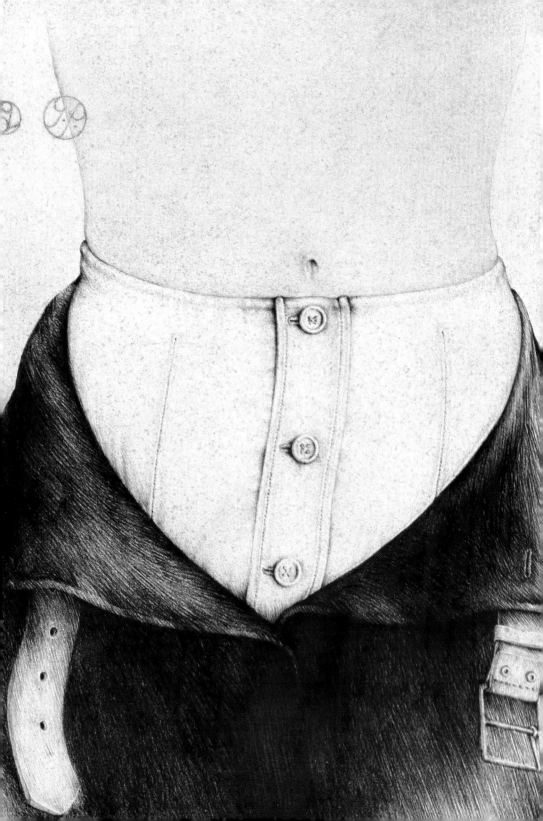

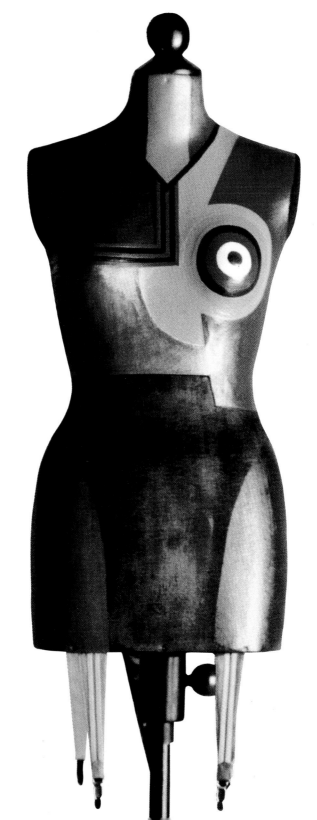

Jean Paul
GAULTIER

Chronology

1991–92	Collection for men 'Le Prisonnier': first show abroad, in Florence, Italy, for Pitti Uomo.
1992	Furniture show at the Galerie VIA.
	First 'Gaultier Jean's' collection.
	Jean-Paul Gaultier retrospective in Los Angeles, in aid of AIDS research (AMFAR).
1992–93	Two collections: 'Les fous de la photographie': homage to the photographic image; and 'Europe de l'avenir': cosmopolitanism and immigrant influences on popular traditions.
1993	Launch of his first fragrance for women 'Jean-Paul Gaultier Haute-Parfumerie'.
	'Les Androjean's' (Androgynes), collection for men: a reinterpretation of some old classics, shown with the new line of 'Gaultier Jean's'.
1993–94	A radical new look for women with the collection 'Les Rabbins chics' ('The Chic Rabbis': homage to the Jewish people): slender lines replacing full busts, curves and cinched waists.
1994	Design of the costumes for Victoria Abril in Pedro Almodóvar's film *Kika*.
	Launch of a new budget-conscious unisex line 'JPG', based on sportswear, replacing the 'Junior Gaultier' range.
	Design of all the costumes for the film *City of Lost Children* by Caro and Jeunet.
1995	Jean-Paul Gaultier retrospective in Vienna, Austria, in aid of AIDS research (Life Ball).
	'Fin de siècle' collection for women: juxtaposition of all the century's different styles in a Dadaist collage (90 percent dresses).
	Launch of first fragrance for men 'Le Mâle'.
1995–96	'Cavaliers, écuyers des temps modernes' ('Horsemen, Modern Riders') collection for men. 'Mad Max' for women.
1996	'Pin-up Boy's' collection for men, in macho and androgynous versions.
	Summer collection 'Cyberbaba'.
1997	'Dim-Dam-Dom' winter collection for women. 'Homme-Couture' ('Couture Man') collection.

Barbès. Collection for women, Autumn/Winter 1984–85. Dress with 'bombshell' breasts in draped orange velvet. Still from a clip from *How to do that?*, directed by Jean-Baptiste Mondino. © Photo Jean-Baptiste Mondino. Right, the same dress, seen by Paolo Roversi. © Photo Paolo Roversi.

Indiscreet charms. 'Le charme coincé de la bourgeoisie'. Collection for women, Autumn/Winter 1985–86. Long quilted 'bedspread' skirt. © Photo Paolo Roversi. **Tarbullboud'deville.** Collection for men, Autumn/Winter 1994–95. Coat in fake panther-fur on wool jersey and black stretch fabric. For the man who is Rasputin, Taras Bulba, Mink de Ville and Buddha all rolled into one. © Paolo Roversi.

Trompe-l'oeil underpant-pants. 'Le Dadaïsme', collection for women, Spring/Summer 1983. *La Mode en Peinture.* © All rights reserved. **Les classiques.** Collection for women, Spring/Summer 1993. Naomi in flesh-coloured catsuit with nude-effect embroidery. © Photo Paolo Roversi.

High Tech. Collection for Autumn/Winter 1980–81, on the theme of salvage and recycling, re-using tins, tea-infusers and printed circuits. Musée Galliera. © Photothèque des Musées de la Ville de Paris. **Invitation card** for the 'Mad Max' collection, Autumn/Winter 1995–96, inspired by electronic circuitry. © Jean-Paul Gaultier.

Constructivist influences. Biker dress of constructivist inspiration in the 'Russe' collection, Autumn/Winter 1986–87. © Photo Foc Kan. **Gaultier and Mad Max.** Padded 'boob' bodice for the finale of the 'Mad Max' collection, Autumn/Winter 1995–96. © Photo Foc Kan.

Tailor's dummy designed by Jean-Paul Gaultier, inspired by the painter Richard Lindner. © Jean-Paul Gaultier, 1990. **'Les Rap'ieuses'.** Naomi Campbell wearing an outfit inspired by Richard Lindner created for 'Les Rap'ieuses' collection. Photo Gilles Bensimon. © SCOOP/*Elle USA*.

Europe of the Future. 'Europe de l'avenir', collection for women, Autumn/Winter 1992–93. Black catsuit in viscose jersey with glove-legs. © Photo Mario Testino. **Barbès.** Collection for women, Autumn/Winter 1984–85. Felt mask hat with 'blue tears', by Stephen Jones for Jean-Paul Gaultier. Illustration by Tony Viramontes, published in *La Mode en Peinture*, 1984. © Photo All rights reserved.

Maid of Orleans. 'Les Tatouages', collection for women, Spring/Summer 1994. Corset dress in cotton tulle, side-laced: homage to Joan of Arc. © Photo Paolo Roversi. **Madonna** photographed in one of the costumes designed for her by Jean-Paul Gaultier for her Blond Ambition world tour in 1990. © Jean-Baptiste Mondino.

Fin de siècle. Collection for women, Spring/Summer 1995. Madonna modelling for Jean-Paul Gaultier. Thirties dress in transparent natural latex with appliquéd gold sequins. © Photo Foc Kan.

Forbidden Gaultier. Left, photo used in the advertising campaign for the 'Forbidden Gaultier' collection, Autumn/Winter 1987–88. © Photo Jean-Paul Gaultier. Right, the same collection for women, 1987–88. Haute couture allied to an outdated view of the future. © Photo Jean-Paul Gaultier.

Mongolia. Androgyny and ethnicity. 'Mongole' collection, Autumn/Winter 1994–95. Photo Jean-Marie Périer. © Scoop/*Elle*, no. 2546, October 1994.

Tattoos on leggings and flesh in 'Les Tatouages', collection for women, Spring/Summer 1994. © Photo Jean-Baptiste Mondino.

Chic Rabbis. 'Les rabbins chics', collection for women, Autumn/Winter 1993–94. 'Homage to the Jewish people', press photo by Jean-Paul Gaultier. © Photo Jean-Paul Gaultier.

Le grand voyage. Collection for women, Autumn/Winter 1994–95. Mongolian influences in this Inuit jacket in reversed wolfskin with trousers in cotton satin. © Photo Catalina Cot (left). © Photo Mikael Jansson (right)/*Vogue* (Paris), 1994.

The circus theme used by Jean-Paul Gaultier to advertise the 'Junior Gaultier' collection, Autumn/Winter 1991–92. © Photo Jean-Paul Gaultier.

Jean-Paul Gaultier in his classic outfit of kilt, sailor top and boots. Photo by Jean-Marie Périer for the 'Spécial Gaultier' issue of *Elle*, 17 October 1994. Photo Jean-Marie Périer. © Scoop/*Elle* no. 2546, October 1994.
Recycling. The tin can, used here as container for Jean-Paul Gaultier fragrance. © Photo Laziz Hamani.

Acknowledgments

The publisher would like to thank the house of Jean-Paul Gaultier for their help in the realization of this work and in particular Donald Potard and Lionel Vermeil.

Thanks also to Jean-Baptiste Mondino, Paolo Roversi, Mario Testino, Jean-Marie Périer, Peter Lindbergh, Marc Hispard, Mikael Janssen, Roxanne Lowit, Mike Ruiz, Hervé Bialé, Catalina Cot, Marcel Hartmann, Gilles Bensimon, Laziz Hamani and Philippe Sebirot.

To Madonna and Liz Rosenberg.

Also to Yvette Horner, Nadia Auerman, Naomi Campbell, Kirsten MacNemany, Christy Turlington, Helena Christensen, Stella Tennant, Claudia Mason, Olga, Christina Valera, Claudia Huidobro, Eugénie Vincent, Elena Nord Borg, Tanel, Devron, Ben Arnold, Vladimir, Nathanaël, Tony Ward, Jérome Le Chevalier and Sébastien Ratto-Viviani.

Finally, this book would have been impossible without the help of Chris and Vincent (Marion de Beaupré), Chris and Vincent (Yannick Morisot), Sandrine (Michele Filomeno), Sylviane and Hortense (Scoop), Liliane Gondel (Phototèque de la Ville de Paris), Catherine Cuckierman and Marie (Éléments); also Sabine Killinger (Élite), Didier (Ford Agency), Jean-Marc (Marilyn Agency), Dominique (FAM), Kathryn Brandt (Turly Production), Karine (Click) and Paola (PH New Men).

We hope they will accept this expression of our sincere gratitude.